THE
BUCK
BOOK

by Anne Akers

SCHOLASTIC INC.
New York Toronto London Auckland Sydney

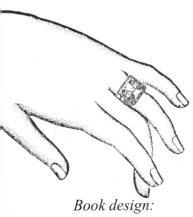

Collage illustrations:
John Craig

Renderings:
Ellery Knight

Book design:
MaryEllen Podgorski & Elizabeth Buchanan

Instructional illustrations, layout and production:
Elizabeth Buchanan

Special thanks to Kate Krislov who laid much of the groundwork for this book.

ISBN 0-590-63493-3

12 11 10 9 8 7 6 5 4 3 2 1   8 9/9 0 1 2 3/0

Printed in the U.S.A.   08

First Scholastic printing, April 1998

Table of Contents

Introduction

The buck. What could be more ordinary? You see it, and promptly spend it every day, with little or no sentimentality. If you were to win a million bucks tomorrow, you would never even think to ask for your prize in ones.

Well, think again, because hidden in every humble bill is a mini-masterpiece waiting to be discovered. And you're just the person to do it. Stunning jewelry, frogs that jump, not-quite-life-size elephants, pleated peacocks: the stuff of fantasies. But don't take my word for it. Find a buck. The newer the better. Then follow the instructions to fold your bill into something amazing. You'll never look at a buck in quite the same way again.

The buck designs that follow are arranged so that the easiest ones come first. Resist the temptation to fold the last one, the Peacock, before you've mastered at least a couple of the easy ones.

WHAT'S THE PYRAMID WITH THE EYE ALL ABOUT?

That pyramid you see on the back of your buck is actually the reverse side of the Great Seal of the United States (the well-known eagle is on the front). The pyramid represents strength and permanence and has been left unfinished to signify the future growth of the country, and its pursuit of perfection. (The original designers were an optimistic bunch.) Look closely and you'll see 1776 printed along the bottom in Roman numerals. The eye surrounded by the sunburst represents the Deity. The Latin translates to "He has favored our undertakings" and "A new order of the ages."

You'll do best if you take the following pointers to heart.

$ In the instructions that follow, <u>finished</u> creases are marked in green. You make a crease by folding the bill and then unfolding it.

$ The red lines on the diagrams show you where your <u>next</u> fold will be.

$ Always start with a new or close-to-new bill—not always an easy task. Ask at the bank. January is the best time to get a supply, as this is when the Treasury issues them.

$ Take the time to make all your folds clean and sharp. It helps to run your thumbnail over the folds every once in awhile. Trust me, this matters.

$ Above all, maintain a sense of humor. I promise, it will help.

Thing$ you could buy for a buck in 1900

Bear Bank

Ladies' Corset

Ladies' Felt Button Boots

BUFFALO BILL BADGE

Buffalo Bill Badge

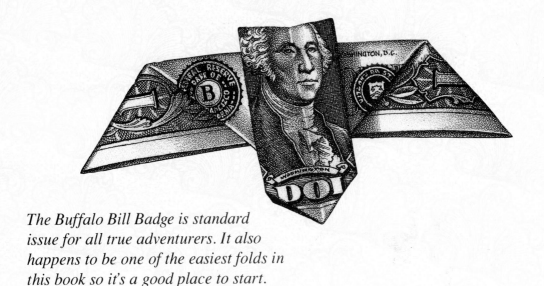

The Buffalo Bill Badge is standard issue for all true adventurers. It also happens to be one of the easiest folds in this book so it's a good place to start.

1. Start with your buck face down. Fold the bottom corners up so the left and right edges are even with the top edge of the bill.

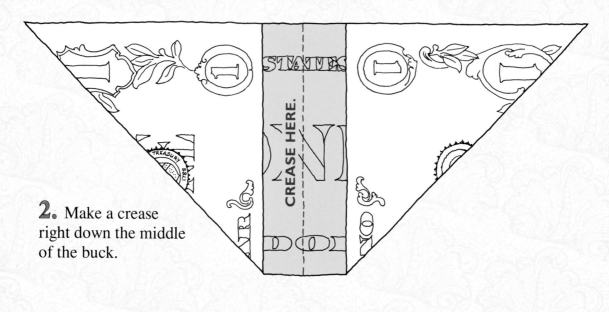

2. Make a crease right down the middle of the buck.

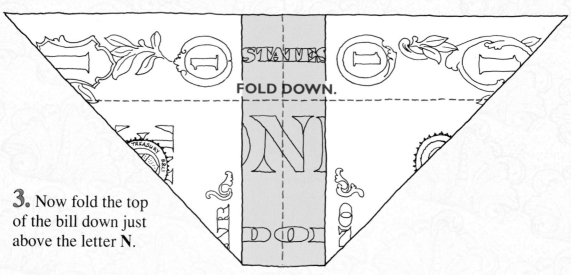

3. Now fold the top of the bill down just above the letter **N**.

Your bill will look like this:

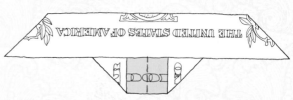

4. To make the wings, fold the right side over to the left along the red dotted line shown in the illustration...

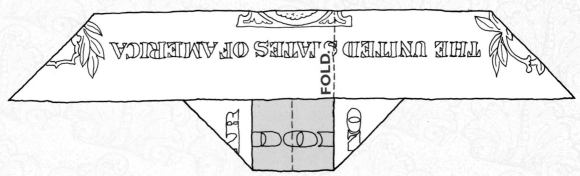

...so it looks like this:

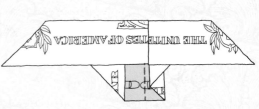

5. Then fold it back along the center line of the bill...

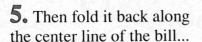

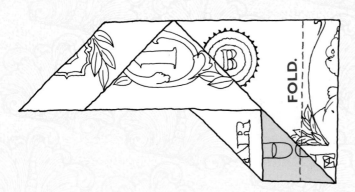

...and you end up with this:

6. Now do the same thing on the left side. Fold the left wing over along the red dotted line...

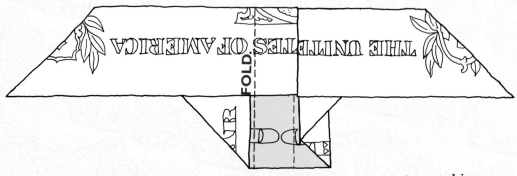

...to get this:

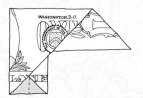

7. Then fold it back along the center line...

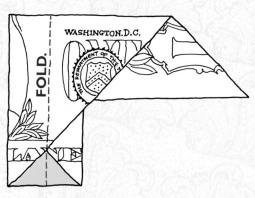

...so it ends up like this:

8. To finish your badge, fold the bottom corners up to make a point. These folds don't have to be exact, they just have to look good.

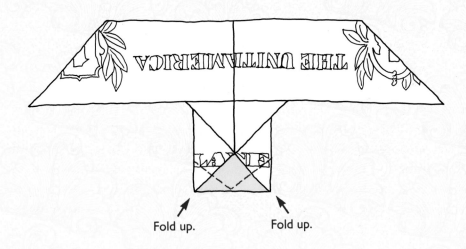

Fold up.   Fold up.

9. Turn the badge over, pin it to your shirt, and you're ready to go!

BOW TIE

Bow Tie

*More than just a
bow tie, this is a truly classic
fashion statement. It's also one of the
few things that can be made with a not-so-new buck.
Even so, try it with a new one your first time through
so you aren't confused by old creases.*

1. Start by making a lengthwise crease down the middle of your bill, then lay it face down in front of you.

2. Fold the top and bottom edges in so they meet at the center crease...

...like this:

3. Now fold the buck in half by bringing the left edge <u>over</u> to the right.

Be sure that all the folds are on the inside and the folded edge is on the left.

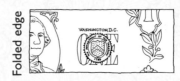

4. Make sharp creases on the dotted lines by folding the corners into the center, then unfolding.

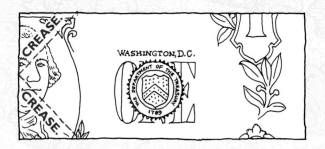

5. The next fold is an inside fold and might seem a little tricky at first. You're going to push the two corners of the buck in so that they meet <u>between</u> the two layers of the bill.

Pushed in.

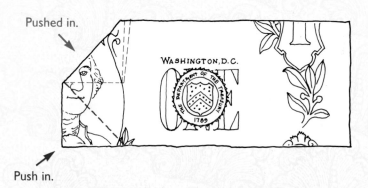

Push in.

You'll end up with a nice, even point with no flaps showing on either side.

The folds are tucked in between the two layers of the bill.

6. Fold the point over to the right as shown in the illustration...

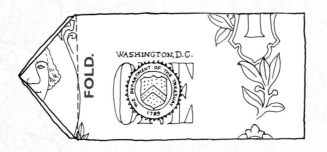

...so it looks like this:

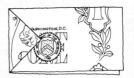

7. Pinch the point against the top layer of the bill, and flip the bottom layer out to the left.

Hold the point against the top layer.

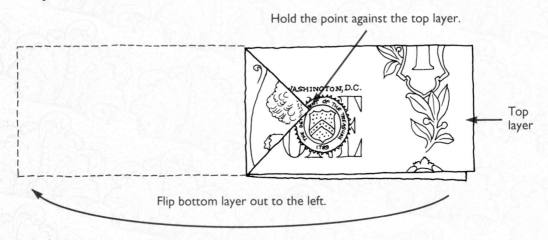

Top layer

Flip bottom layer out to the left.

Before you go on, make sure your buck looks like this:

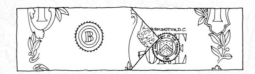

8. Keep the point right where it is, and fold the left end over to the right so the edges of the bill meet and the point is sandwiched between the two layers.

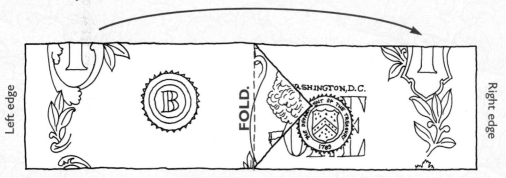

It will look like this, with the point tucked between the two layers of the bill.

9. Now, working with the <u>top layer</u> only, fold the corners on the left side in so they meet in the center.

Top layer

Like this:

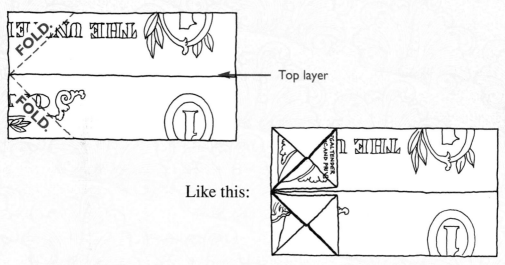

10. Turn the bill over and make the same fold on the bottom layer.

You end up with this:

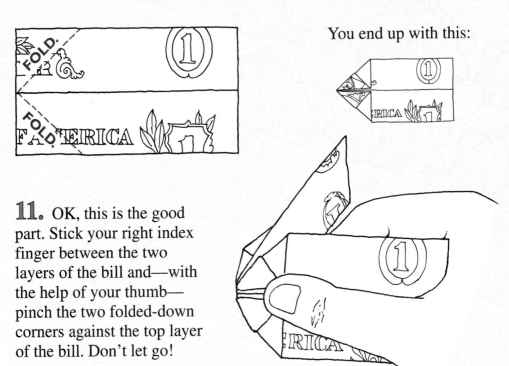

11. OK, this is the good part. Stick your right index finger between the two layers of the bill and—with the help of your thumb— pinch the two folded-down corners against the top layer of the bill. Don't let go!

12. Now do the same thing with the bottom layer, using your left hand. Once you've got everything under control, pull your hands apart a bit so the bill lies flat.

Smooth these new folds out so it's all very flat.

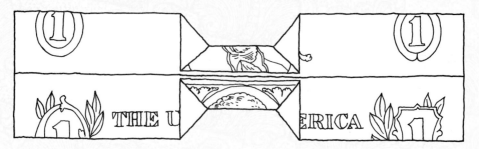

13. Turn your buck over. George should be looking right at you from the center of the bow.

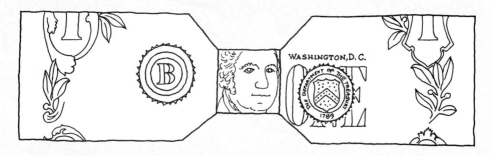

14. You can leave your bow tie as it is or, for a more natural look, flare the corners out a bit (this is the part that is a little easier if you're using an old bill).

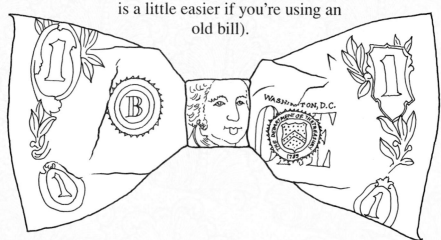

DOLLAR RING

Dollar Ring

The Dollar Ring is a classic and should be in everyone's buck-folding repertoire. The result is a kid-sized ring or an adult pinkie ring.

If you want something a little larger, you'll do better with the Dime-in-Ring.

1. Start with the usual crisp dollar bill. Fold the bottom edge up so that just the back bottom margin shows. You'll notice that the back margins are a little bigger than those on the front. Don't panic. This is as it should be.

2. Now fold the top half down to cover the flap you've just made. Leave it short of the bottom edge by just a hair.

Like this:

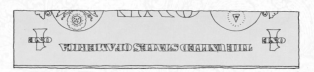

3. Fold the top half down again. This time it should end up exactly even with the bottom edge.

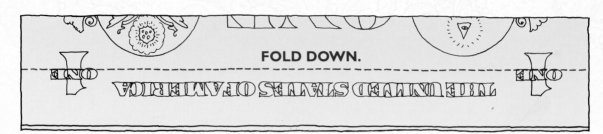

You get this:

4. Turn the bill over and fold the right margin under...

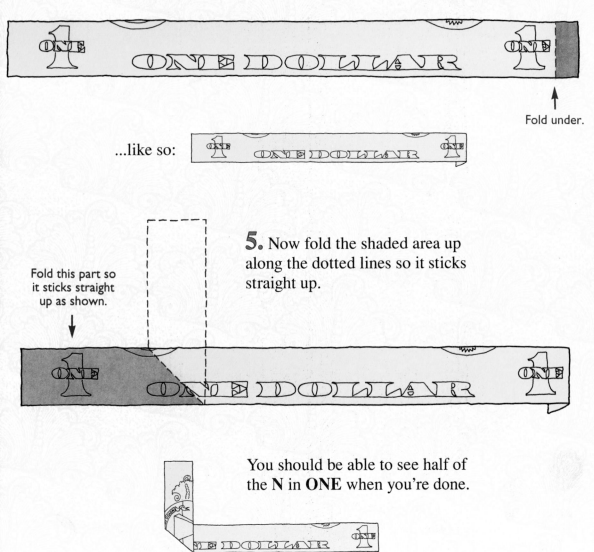

Fold under.

...like so:

5. Now fold the shaded area up along the dotted lines so it sticks straight up.

Fold this part so it sticks straight up as shown.

You should be able to see half of the **N** in **ONE** when you're done.

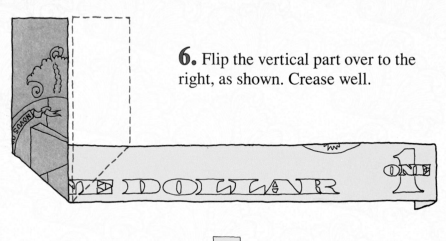

6. Flip the vertical part over to the right, as shown. Crease well.

Your buck should look like this now:

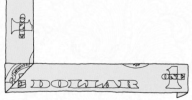

7. This next fold is optional, but it will make your finished ring a little nicer. Taper the top and bottom edges of the bill a bit by folding the top and bottom edges in.

FOLD.

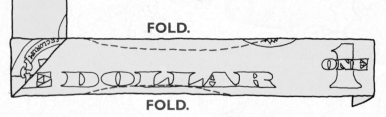

FOLD.

Run a pencil over these folds to really flatten them.

8. Turn the bill over and hold it in your left hand. Wrap it back around your index finger so the eagle ends up upside down right under the vertical flap.

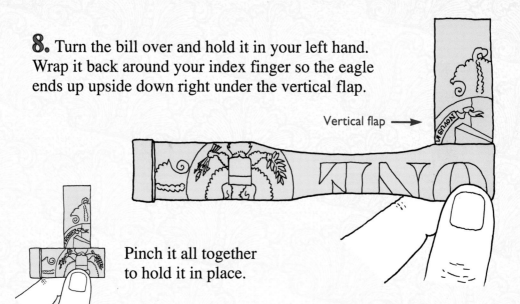

Vertical flap →

Pinch it all together to hold it in place.

9. Now fold the vertical flap down...

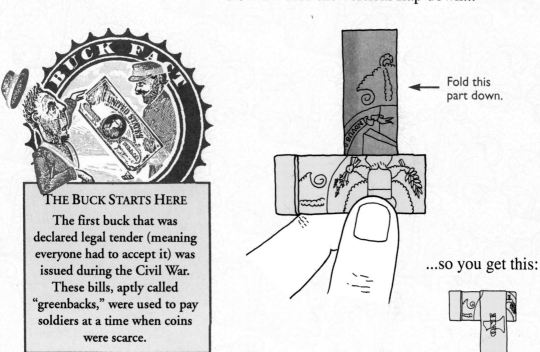

← Fold this part down.

THE BUCK STARTS HERE

The first buck that was declared legal tender (meaning everyone had to accept it) was issued during the Civil War. These bills, aptly called "greenbacks," were used to pay soldiers at a time when coins were scarce.

...so you get this:

10. Next, fold the flap on the left across the front of the ring.

Fold over.

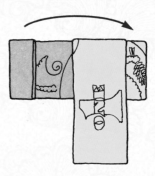

If the **1** isn't centered, you've been a little sloppy. Back up a few steps and adjust.

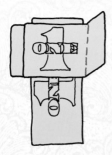

11. To keep the **1** from popping up, tuck the little folded-over edge under the vertical flap.

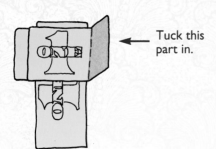

← Tuck this part in.

BUCK FACT

HOW MUCH DO YOU KNOW ABOUT MONEY?

Bills are only printed in seven denominations. Try to name them all before you turn the page for the answer. For the grand prize, name the man that appears on each one.

12. Finally, turn the ring over so you can see the inside. There will be a diagonal slot behind the **1**. Tuck the flap (the shaded area in the illustration) into this slot.

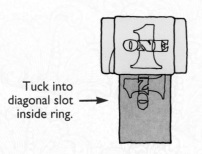

Tuck into diagonal slot inside ring. →

ANSWER

$1 - George Washington
$2 - Thomas Jefferson
$5 - Abraham Lincoln
$10 - Alexander Hamilton
$20 - Andrew Jackson
$50 - Ulysses S. Grant
$100 - Benjamin Franklin

Very nice. Wear it with pride.

DIME-IN-RING

Dime-in-Ring

This ring is suitable for more formal occasions:

black-tie dinners, weddings—you know what I'm talking about.

1. As always, you'll need a crisp new bill for this one. Starting with the bill face up, fold it in half lengthwise, then unfold. You should have a good clean crease running the length of the bill.

2. Now fold the top and bottom edges in so they meet at this center crease.

Your buck will
look like this:

3. Make two more lengthwise creases by folding the top and bottom edges into the center. Run your thumbnail along these folds to make them really sharp before you unfold them.

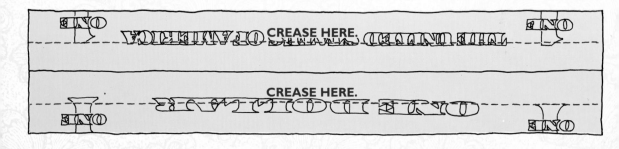

4. Now fold your buck in half as shown, bringing the right edge <u>back</u> to meet the left edge.

All the folds will be on the outside.

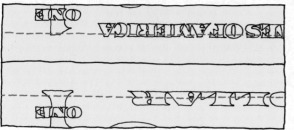

This is the folded edge.

5. This next fold is a <u>two-step</u> fold. Make sharp creases on the dotted lines by folding the corners in to the center crease. Remember, to make a crease you have to fold and unfold.

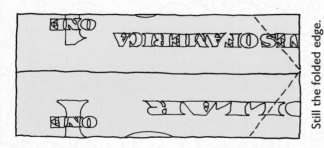

Still the folded edge.

BUCK FACT

MONEY COMES WITH A MONEY-BACK GUARANTEE

Should you inadvertently burn, shred, soak or otherwise mutilate your money, the kind people in the Office of Currency Standards in Washington, D.C. will sort through the remains in search of redeemable money. If they can account for 51% of a bill, they'll give you a replacement. These folks have seen it all: burned mattresses, moldy money, unburied treasure. In one noteworthy case, several hundred dollars were retrieved from the belly of one very unhappy cow.

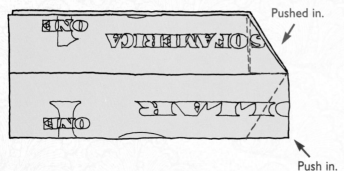

Pushed in.

Push in.

6. Now, push the two corners in so they meet <u>between</u> the two layers of the bill. If this doesn't work well, go back and make sure the folds in step 5 are really sharp.

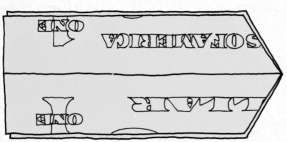

If you've done these two "push-in folds" right, you'll have a smooth point on the folded end of the bill.

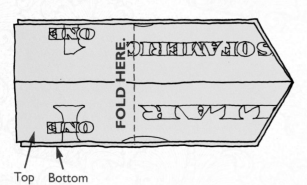

FOLD HERE.

Top   Bottom

7. Look at your bill and confirm that there are two layers: the top and the bottom. In the next few steps, you'll only be working with the <u>top</u> layer. Fold <u>just the top layer</u> as shown.

You'll end up with this:

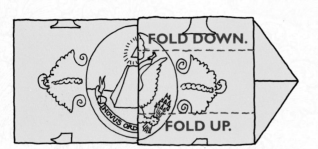

FOLD DOWN.

FOLD UP.

8. Still working with the top layer, fold the top and bottom edges in to the center...

...so your buck looks like this:

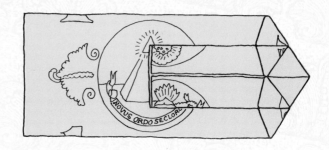

9. Now turn the bill over so you can work on the bottom layer. Fold the edges in to the center...

FOLD DOWN HERE.

FOLD UP HERE.

...so you get this:

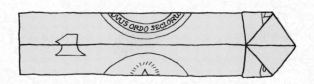

10. Turn the bill over again, and make sure it matches the illustration. If it does, take a deep breath and carry on. If not, go back a few steps to find out where you went wrong.

11. This next step will make the ring band and dime box. Put the buck down in front of you. Hold the bottom layer down and flip the top layer over as shown.

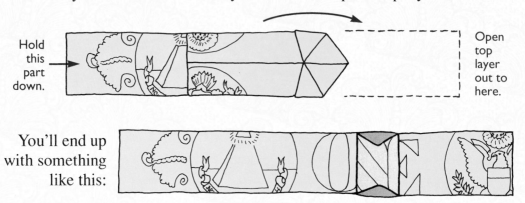

You'll end up with something like this:

The dime box will look a little smooshed, so use the eraser end of a pencil or your finger to shape it into a neat square little box with a flat bottom, like so:

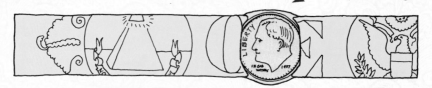

12. Once you've got the box in good shape, drop a dime into it. Crimp the edges down a little to hold the dime in place.

Crimp these edges down.

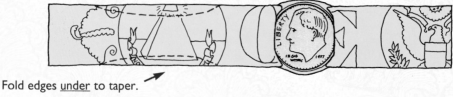

13. If you want to taper the ring band like you did for the Dollar Ring (p. 24), now's the time. Again, this is optional, but it will make the ring a little nicer.

Fold edges <u>under</u> to taper.

Run a pencil over these folds to flatten them.

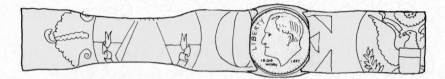

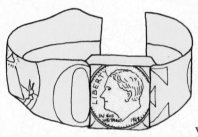

14. Curve the buck into a ring and tuck the long end into the folds of the short end. Go ahead and cheat a little by tapering the long end so it tucks in easier. If you really want to cheat, and you'll probably have to, use a little tape to keep the band fastened.

If the ring is too big for you, fold the long end to make it shorter before you tuck it into the other end.

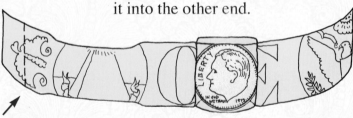

Fold here to make
the ring smaller.

YOWZA! Never take this ring apart; you'll never need a buck that badly.

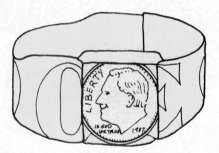

JUMPING FROG

Jumping Frog

With a little help, this frog will actually hop around just like a real one. Sort of.

1. Start with your buck face up. Fold the top right corner down to the bottom edge, crease it well and unfold. Now fold the bottom corner up to the top edge, crease and unfold.

2. These two creases will criss-cross to make an **X**. Fold the right edge of the bill over toward the center, making sure this new fold runs right through the center of the **X**.

3. Now make one of those tricky inside folds by pushing the corners in so they meet <u>between</u> the two layers of the bill.

Pushed in.

Push in.

You'll end up with a smooth point on the front and on the back.

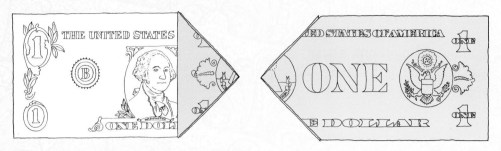

4. Fold the left edge of the bill over so that it meets the right edge.

Like this:

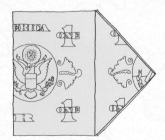

NOW HERE'S A REAL BARGAIN

It costs a mere 4.1 cents to make a $1 bill.
Of course if you want a real bargain, go for
the $100 bill: It costs just the same.

5. Now, make diagonal creases on the left side of the bill by folding the corners in to the center and then unfolding them. These creases should be really sharp—it will make it easier later.

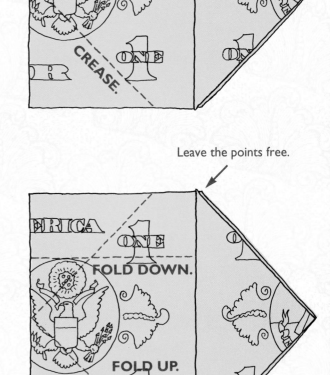

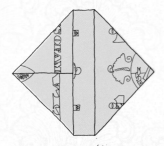

Fold the corners in like this, then unfold.

6. Go back to the pointed end of the buck. Notice that it is made up of two layers. Fold the top and bottom edges of the bill in to the center, being careful not to fold the top layer of the point.

Leave the points free.

Bottom layer

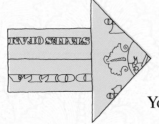

Your bill should look like this.

7. Now fold the flat end of the buck over to the right...

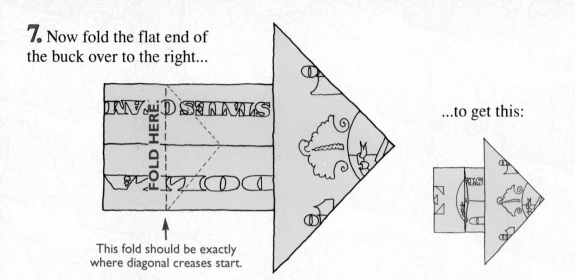

...to get this:

This fold should be exactly where diagonal creases start.

8. Look closely at the flap you've just folded over. Find the two corners that meet just <u>under</u> the folded edge (we've marked them with red dots). Pinch the bill on the **E** to hold this fold in place. Now pull the corners out—one at a time—so they extend out beyond the body of the frog and make its legs.

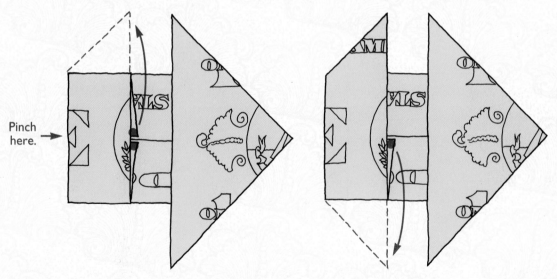

Pinch here.

You may have to work a little to make these folds look right. Once they do, press them down flat. Really flat. If you have problems making these folds, go back to step 6 and sharpen the creases a bit.

9. To shape the back legs, fold them back along the crease lines you've already made.

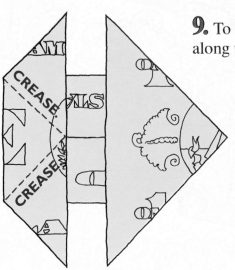

You'll end up with this:

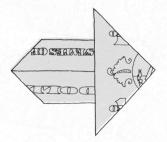

10. Now fold the legs back out on the red dotted lines.

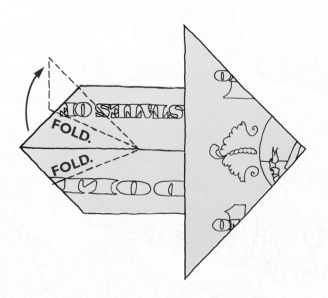

Your buck should be looking more like a frog now.

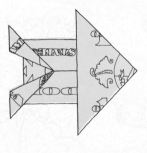

11. Go back to the pointy end of the bill. Fold the front legs forward on the dotted lines. These folds don't have to be exact, they just have to make good frog legs.

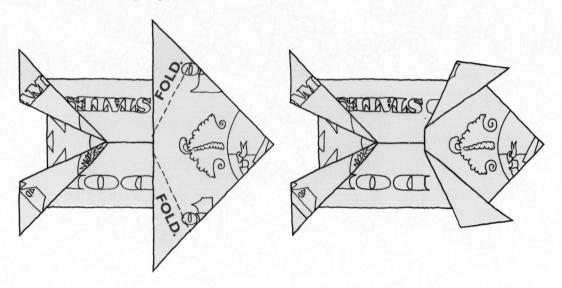

12. OK, now turn your frog over. The next two folds are the ones that will make your frog jump. They're also the only two that you <u>don't</u> want to press too flat. Fold the whole frog in half—backwards toward the feet. Make this fold right down the middle of the **N**...

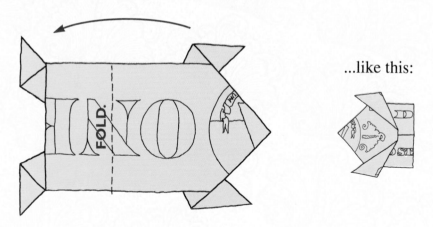

...like this:

13. Now fold the head back where it came from, this time making the fold run through the **D** in **DOLLAR**.

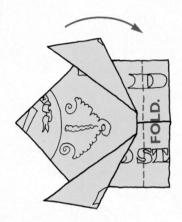

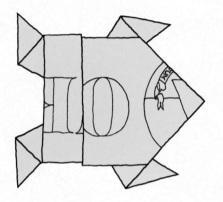

Your frog should have a nice zig-zag in its body (the better to jump with!). Remember, don't press these folds too flat.

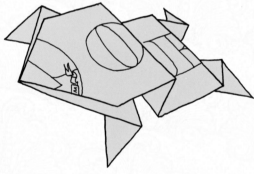

WOULD YOU LIKE THAT STARCHED?

Back in 1916, you could return dirty money to Washington to be laundered. If the money was in good enough shape, it would be washed, ironed and reissued.

14. To make your frog jump, rest one finger <u>lightly</u> on its rear. Slide your finger back while pressing down gently. When your finger slips off the frog, it will take a little leap forward. The key is to use a <u>very</u> light touch.

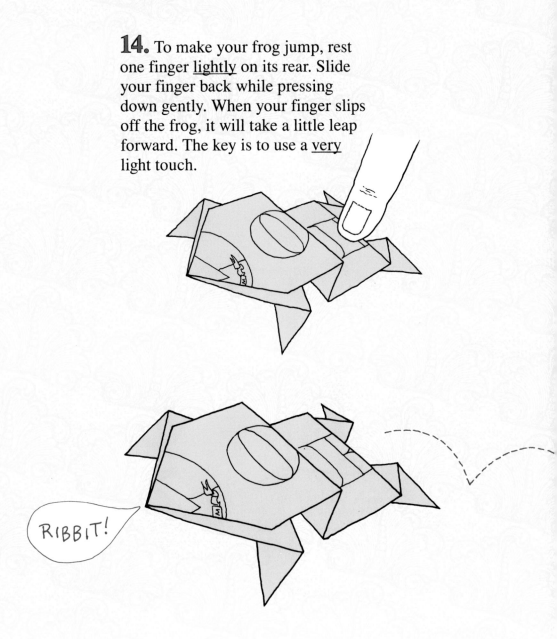

RIBBIT!

ELEPHANT

Elephant

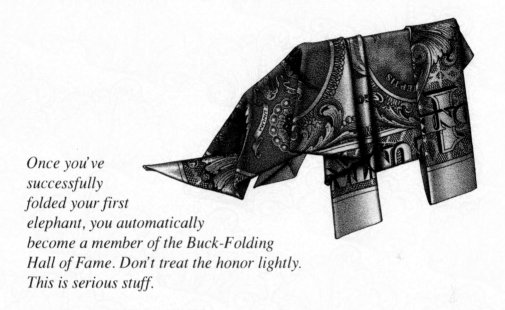

*Once you've
successfully
folded your first
elephant, you automatically
become a member of the Buck-Folding
Hall of Fame. Don't treat the honor lightly.
This is serious stuff.*

1. Fold your buck in half lengthwise, then unfold it so you have a nice sharp crease. Fold the left-hand corners in to this crease to make a point.

2. Fold again along the dotted lines to make a long skinny point.

3. Now, fold the bill so the point just touches the other end of the bill.

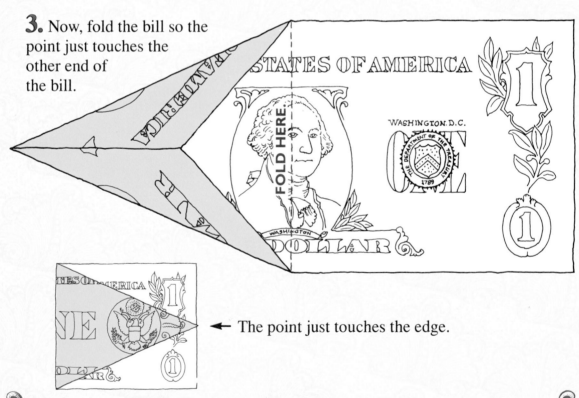

← The point just touches the edge.

4. Turn the bill over so the point is on the underside. Fold <u>just the top layer</u> in half, crease it well, then unfold.

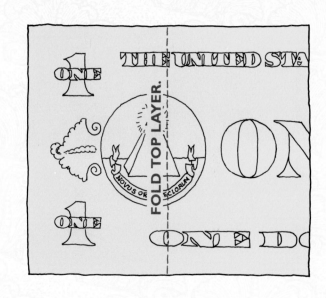

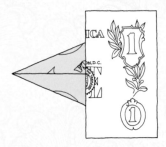

Fold the bill like this to make a sharp crease.

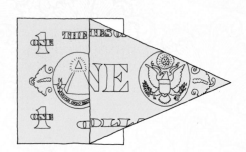

5. Find the folded edge of the bill. Fold this edge over so it meets the crease you just made. As you make this fold, flip the point back around to the front...

...so it looks like this:

Folded edge

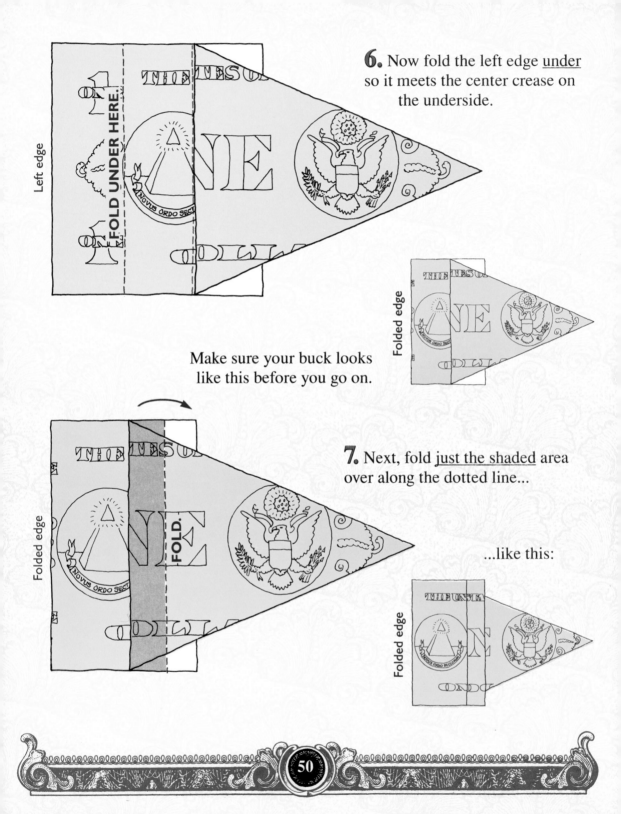

6. Now fold the left edge <u>under</u> so it meets the center crease on the underside.

Left edge

FOLD UNDER HERE.

Folded edge

Make sure your buck looks like this before you go on.

Folded edge

FOLD.

7. Next, fold <u>just the shaded</u> area over along the dotted line...

...like this:

Folded edge

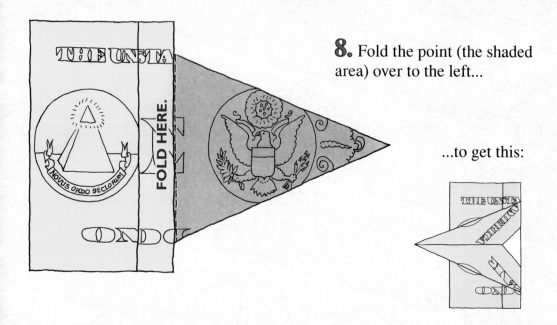

8. Fold the point (the shaded area) over to the left...

...to get this:

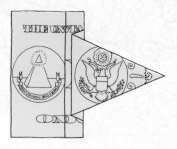

9. Then fold the shaded area back to the right to make a little fan fold.

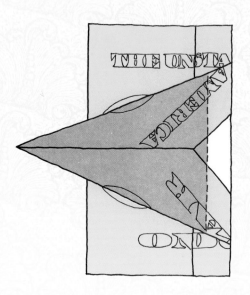

Notice that this fold is a little narrower than the one it sits on top of.

You've just made the front legs and head of the elephant.

10. To make the back legs, fold the flat end (this is a folded edge) over so it meets that same center crease you made in step 4. At the same time, flip the left edge of the bill back around to the front.

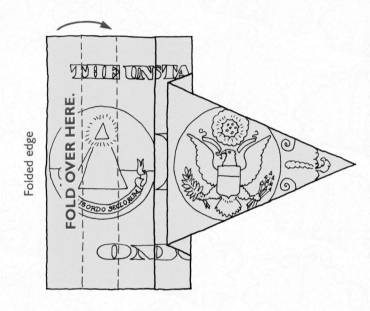

Folded edge

FOLD OVER HERE.

Check that your buck looks just like this before you go on.

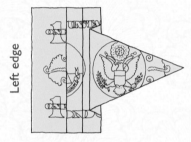

Left edge

BUCK FACT

PURE SILVER

11. Turn the buck over. It should look like this:

Take a minute to run your fist over the whole thing to flatten all the folds.

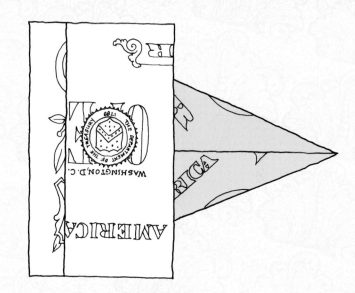

12. The next few steps shape the legs. This part can get a little tricky, so take it slowly. Notice the rectangle that makes up the body of the elephant. Fold all four corners of this rectangle in, as shown, crease them well, then unfold. <u>Be careful to fold only the top layer of the rectangle</u>.

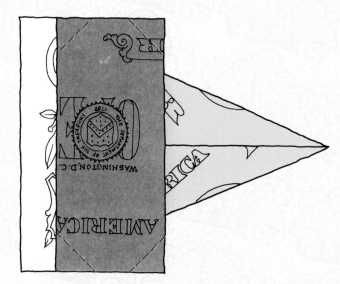

Fold the corners down to look like this, then unfold.

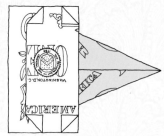

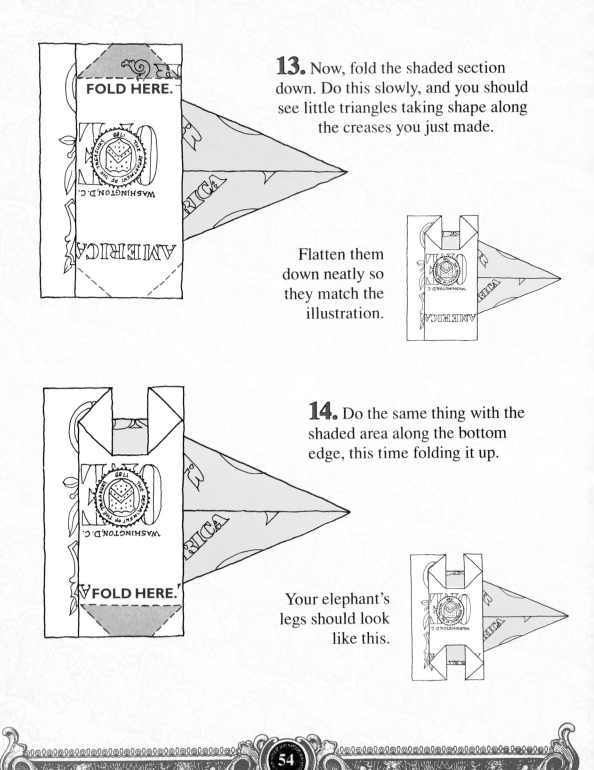

13. Now, fold the shaded section down. Do this slowly, and you should see little triangles taking shape along the creases you just made.

Flatten them down neatly so they match the illustration.

14. Do the same thing with the shaded area along the bottom edge, this time folding it up.

Your elephant's legs should look like this.

15. Fold the left edge of the bill over to make a crease that runs right along the back border. You're only making a crease here, so don't forget to unfold.

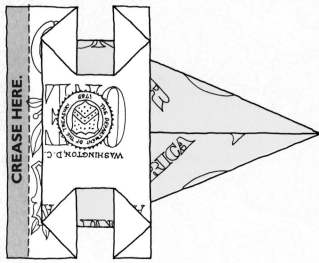

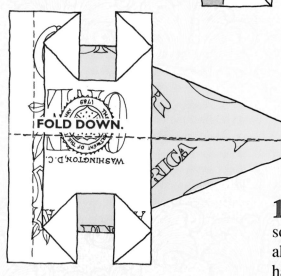

16. You're probably ready for something easy by now, so go ahead and fold the elephant in half. All the folds you've made will be on the inside.

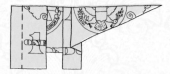

If you can't see the beginnings of an elephant by now, you're not trying hard enough.

17. This next fold isn't really a precise one. It's one of those "just-make-it-look-right" folds. In this case anything that ends up resembling a tail is right.

Find the red dot we've marked on the elephant's hind legs. Fold the left border back <u>inside</u> the elephant along the crease lines but only fold up to the red dot. Leave the part above the dot poking out to make the tail.

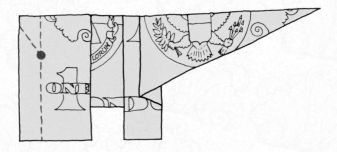

Do what you can to make your elephant look like this.

WHAT HAPPENS TO BEAT-UP BUCKS?

When bucks finally wear out, they're sent back to the nearest Federal Reserve bank, where they're run through a machine that sorts out the good, the bad and the counterfeit. The counterfeit bills are sent on to the Secret Service for investigation. The tired bills are first pulverized and then buried, sometimes in the local landfill. Until a couple of years ago, these bills were incinerated, but because of the lead used in the ink, burning bucks has become an environmental no-no.

18. The ears are shaped by making a little pleat in the pointed section. To do this, pinch the elephant's front legs together, then swing the pointed end down a bit, allowing it to push <u>between the two layers</u> of the body just slightly.

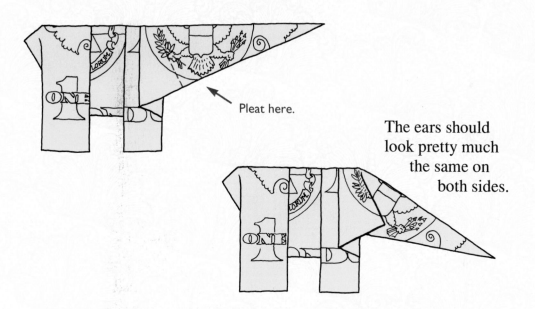

Pleat here.

The ears should look pretty much the same on both sides.

19. You're almost there now, so don't give up! Pinch the ears together and open up the trunk section so it's flat in front.

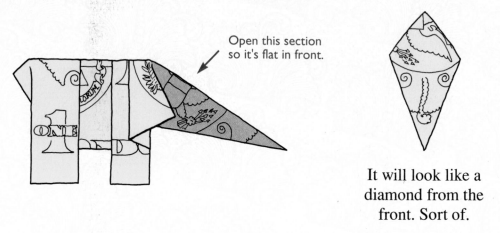

Open this section so it's flat in front.

It will look like a diamond from the front. Sort of.

20. Fold the point up, stopping just before it sticks straight up. Pinch the trunk and head back together again.

Pull trunk up to here...

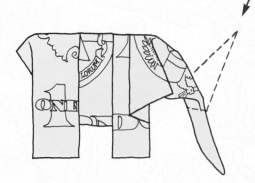

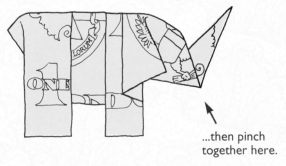

...then pinch together here.

The trunk should angle up nicely now.

21. You can stop here or make one more tiny pleated fold so the trunk curves back.

One Business that Always Makes Money

All U.S. currency is printed at the Bureau of Printing and Engraving in either Washington, D.C. or Ft. Worth, Texas. Between the 16 presses at the two plants, they can churn out 2.5 million bills a day. Not a bad day's work, especially when $100 bills are being printed.

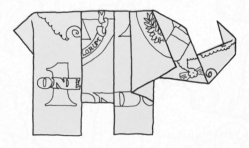

22. Your elephant will stand up better if you push a paper clip up into one of its back legs.

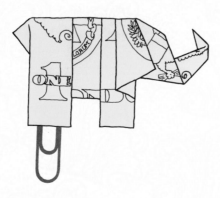

Very impressive.

PEACOCK

SERENADE
BIRD
SEED

Peacock

This is your final exam—the best-looking, most complicated fold in the book. Master some of the easier folds before you step up to this one.

One last bit of advice: More than ever before, you have to press all the folds flat as you go. Really flat. It will turn out much better if you do.

1. Make diagonal creases as shown. To do this fold the top corner down to the bottom edge, crease and unfold, then fold the bottom corner up to the top edge, crease and unfold. These creases have to be sharper than sharp, so use your thumbnail to really flatten them.

2. Now fold the left end of the bill over. This fold should run exactly through the center of the **X** made by the two creases in step 1.

3. Make an inside fold by pushing the two corners in so they meet <u>between</u> the two layers of the bill.

Pushed in.

Push in. →

Your bill will look like this, with all the flaps tucked in between the top and bottom layer of the buck.

4. Look at your bill and find the triangle that we've shaded in the illustration. You're only going to be working with the <u>top</u> flaps of this triangle for now.

5. Crease the triangle by folding the points into the center as shown. Make these creases really sharp, then unfold them.

You'll end up with two new creases in your triangle.

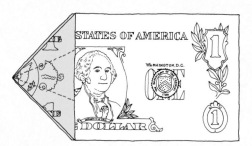

THE BUCKS ARE COMING!

Paul Revere gets credit for engraving the plates for the first paper money printed in the U.S. This "Continental Currency" was just one of many kinds of money floating around at a time when banks could print their own. Most people preferred gold or silver coins to the paper stuff.

6. Now make another good crease by folding the triangle (top flap only!) in half. First fold the top down to the bottom (fold point A down to point B), crease and unfold...

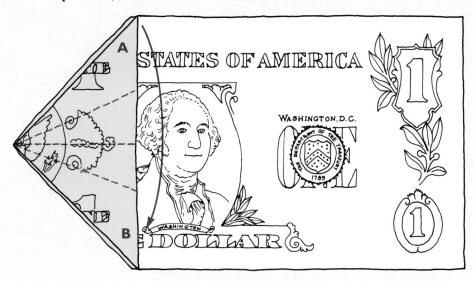

...then fold the bottom up to the top (fold point B up to point A), crease and unfold. Your buck will end up looking just like it did at the end of step 5, but with a new crease running through the triangle.

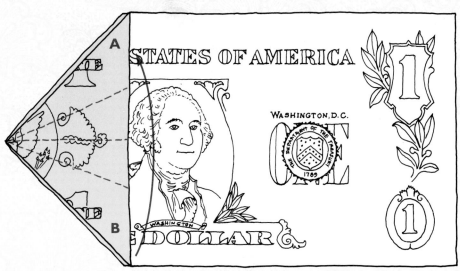

7. This next step is a little complicated, so take it slowly and don't give up. Hold the lower flap of the triangle in place. Find the point on your buck that we've marked with a red dot in the illustration. Lift this flap (we've shaded it) so that it sticks straight up from the bill and looks kind of like a sail.

Hold this section down.

Now flatten this same shaded section by pushing the red dot down so it sits right on top of the green dot. You'll get this:

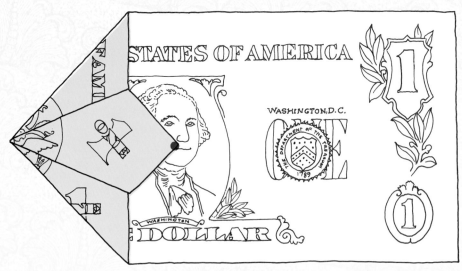

8. Find the red dot again—it's still in the same place. Fold this dot up so it sits on top of the black dot, but don't press this section flat just yet.

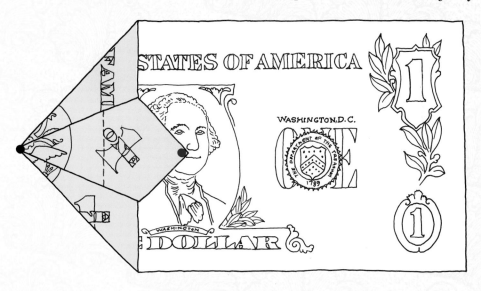

The folded-up section will look like this:

9. Now use a sharp pencil to neaten these folds as shown.

Smooth all the folds flat so they match the illustration. Don't be discouraged if you don't get this fold right the first time—few people do. The illustration is your best guide here, so check it carefully before you go on.

10. Once you've got these folds right, and they're pressed really flat, fold the red dot back down to the green one again...

...like this:

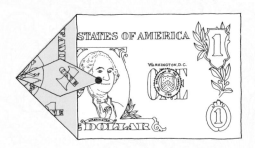

MONEY ON THE HOOF

Back before the days of paper money, Americans traded buckskins, hence the name "bucks." Imagine the thrill you'd feel after winning the 1772 lottery and taking home a million bucks.

11. Now fold the shaded section in half, bottom to top.

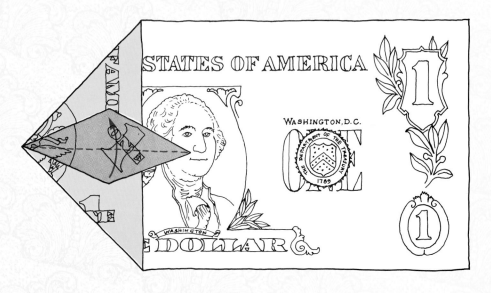

You've just made a leg.

12. OK, now you have to make all the same folds on the bottom half of the triangle. We've shaded this section to make it easier. Remember, you're only working with the top flap here.

Lift the shaded part of the triangle so it points straight up, then press it flat so that the red dot lines up with the green dot.

Like this:

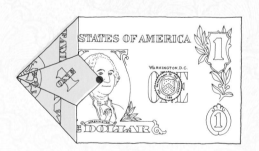

FUNNY MONEY

The Secret Service was originally set up in 1865 to combat widespread counterfeiting. It was estimated that one-third of the money in circulation at that time was phony.

13. Now fold the red dot up so it sits on top of the black dot. Again, this will be a little messy...

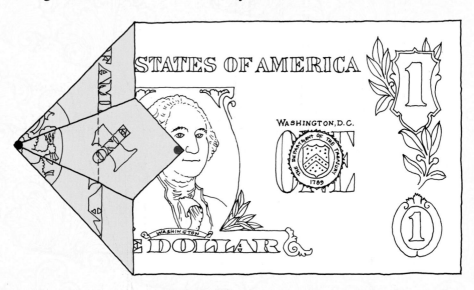

...but use a pencil like you did in step 9 to neaten the folds. Make sure you end up with this:

Press these folds really flat.

14. Fold the red dot back down to the green dot.

Like so:

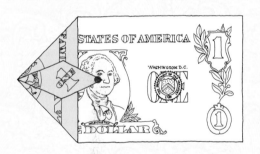

WOULD YOU LIKE SOME HELP TO YOUR CAR WITH THAT?

Imagine, if you will, the following nightmare: You're locked in a mall with a billion bucks and you can't come home until all your money is spent. If you're really good, and you find a way to spend $200 a minute, every minute of every day, you'd make it home in just under ten years.

15. Then fold the shaded section along the dotted line, this time folding the top half down to the bottom.

Be careful that you fold just this one section. The first leg stays in its place.

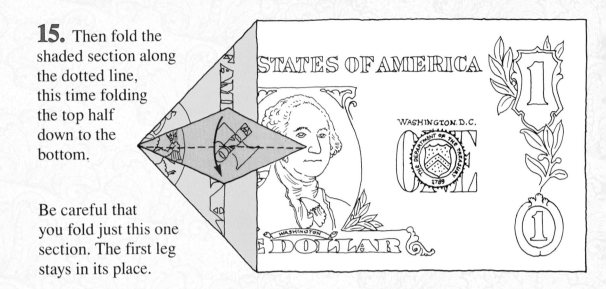

You should end up with this:

16. Next, fold the shaded area to the left along the dotted line.

Smoosh it all really flat before you go on.

17. You're almost through the worst of it now, so hang in there. Fold the bottom layer of the bill along the dotted lines. Be careful to tuck these flaps under all the folds you've just made.

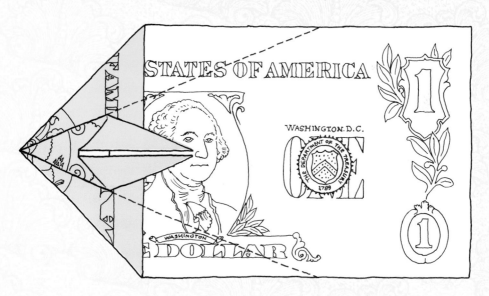

You'll get this:

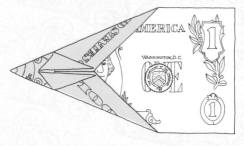

18. Now fold the legs out as shown.

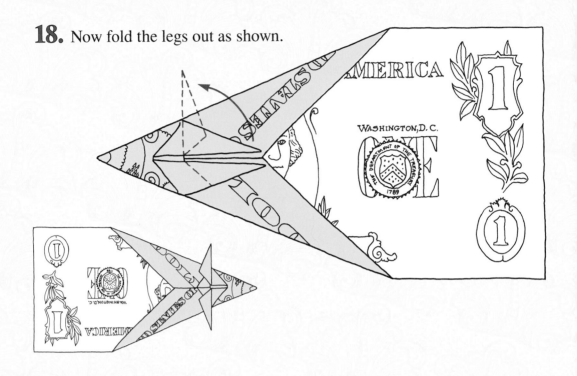

19. Take a deep breath, and congratulate yourself. You've finished the hardest part. Fold the bill in half so that all your folds are on the inside.

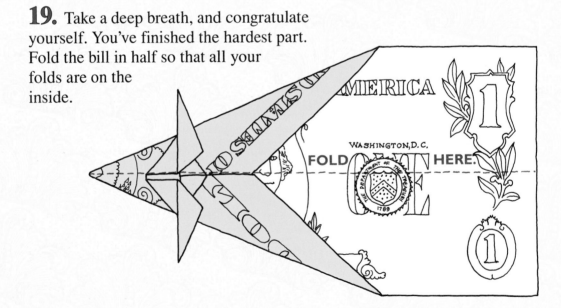

FOLD HERE.

Your buck should be looking
more like a peacock now.

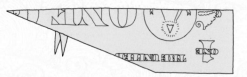

20. Fold the tail on the dotted line so it hangs straight down.

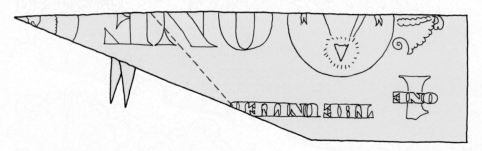

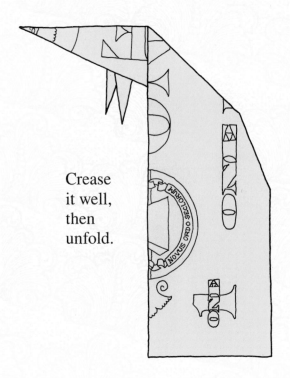

Crease
it well,
then
unfold.

MT. MONEY

If you made a stack of just the
worn $1 bills that are destroyed in
a single year, the stack would
tower 200 miles into the sky. Mt.
Everest is a mere five miles tall.
There's a thought to keep you
awake at night.

21. Open the peacock up again and lay it down flat in front of you. This time lay it belly down.

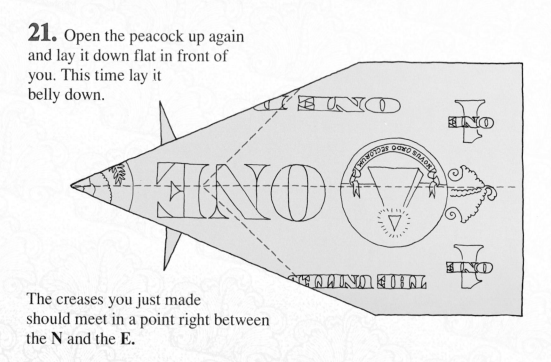

The creases you just made should meet in a point right between the **N** and the **E**.

22. The tail is made up of lots of little fan folds. Start by folding the shaded area under...

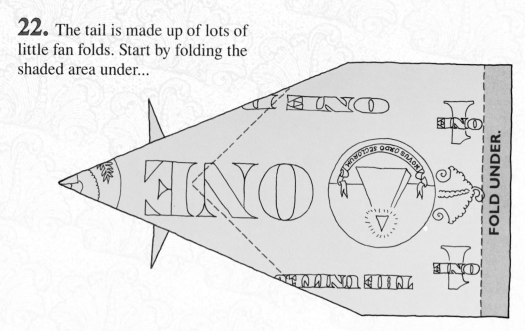

FOLD UNDER.

...then fold it back over to the front as shown.

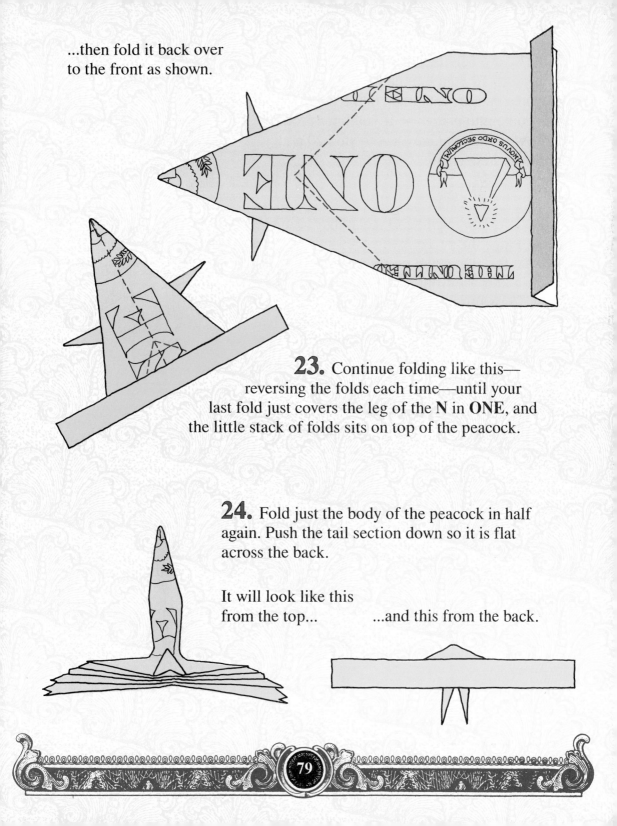

23. Continue folding like this—reversing the folds each time—until your last fold just covers the leg of the **N** in **ONE**, and the little stack of folds sits on top of the peacock.

24. Fold just the body of the peacock in half again. Push the tail section down so it is flat across the back.

It will look like this from the top...

...and this from the back.

25. Now pinch the tail section together so it sticks straight out the back. Those diagonal creases you made in the body will come into play now. If you have problems with this fold, go back to step 20 and improve these creases.

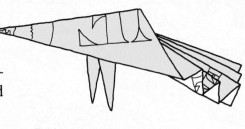

Fold pointy end up here.

26. Next you're going to make the neck. Pinch the peacock together just over its feet. Open the pointy end out so it's flat in the front and bend it up a little. Press this new fold—actually more of a tuck—flat. This might be a little harder than usual because you're folding so many layers.

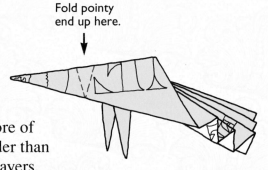

The point should angle up.

27. Pinch the neck right where it turns upward, and pull just a little bit of the point down...

...to make a head.

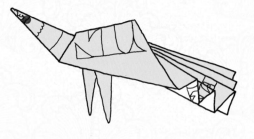

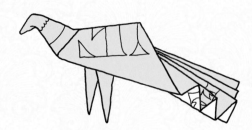

28. Now make a
little forward fold in
the legs to give your
peacock feet.

29. You can leave your
peacock like this, or lift the
tail up so it fans in its full
glory. Either way, you'll probably
want to tape the two halves of the tail
together so it looks like one piece.

Amazing. Don't let
anyone ever accuse
you of lacking talent.

Credits

Buck fold designs:

Buffalo Bill Badge	Bill Caruba
Dime-in-Ring	Kenneth Kawamura
Jumping Frog	Robert Neale
Elephant	Neal Elias
Peacock	Simplification of a design by Adolfo Cerceda